Douglas W. Knighton earned a BA from Wheaton College and a Masters of Divinity from Fuller Theological Seminary. He served as a regional director for the Christian Medical and Dental Society for ten years. Knighton lives with his wife, Maja, and their three children in Naperville, Illinois.

The Kingdom of Heaven Is like . . . a Doctor and a Patient

Douglas W. Knighton

Baker Books

A Division of Baker Book House Co
Grand Rapids, Michigan 49516

© 1997 by Douglas W. Knighton

Published by Baker Books
a division of Baker Book House Company
P.O. Box 6287, Grand Rapids, MI 49516-6287

Printed in the United States of America

Library of Congress Cataloging-in-Publication Data

Knighton, Douglas W., 1947–
    The kingdom of heaven is like . . . a doctor and a patient / Douglas
W. Knighton.
        p.   cm.
      ISBN 0-8010-5379-X (paper)
      1. Christian life. 2. Physician and patient. I. Title.
BV4501.2.K545   1997
248.4—dc20   96-26101

Scripture quotations not otherwise identified are from the New American
Standard Bible®, © The Lockman Foundation 1960, 1962, 1963, 1968, 1971,
1972, 1973, 1975, 1977, 1995. Used by permission.

Scripture verses identified DWK are the author's translation.

Contents

Prologue

"It is not those who are healthy who need a physician, but those who are sick. I did not come to call the righteous, but sinners" (Mark 2:17).

"If you keep My commandments, you will abide in My love" (John 15:10).

N early twenty years ago, a friend introduced me to an analogy he had found helpful in thinking about our relationship with Jesus Christ. It seems to highlight some aspects of that relationship better than the more common analogies we encounter in Scripture. Although we often talk in terms of the Father-child relationship or the King-subject relationship because the Bible uses this terminology frequently, Dan Fuller taught me to relate to Christ as a patient relates to a doctor.

The threads of this analogy are woven throughout Scripture. From beginning to end, God presents himself as one who prescribes ways of living that will result in either physical or spiritual healing, or both. He describes himself as one who initiates and performs the work necessary for our return to health. When he delivered Israel from Egypt, the Eternal One who spoke with Moses proclaimed his uniqueness in terms of healing: "There is no god besides Me . . . it is I who heal" (Deut. 32:39). God said through Jeremiah that our hearts are incurably ill with wickedness (Jer. 17:9), and promised through Ezekiel to take out those stony hearts and replace them with new hearts (Ezek. 36:26). Even in our sin, God says that through the Messiah's sufferings we would find healing (Isa. 53:5). So we are not surprised when Jesus speaks in the same terms. He says that it is not the healthy who need a physician, but the sick, and that he did not come to call the righteous, but sinners (Mark 2:17). The Lord *wants* his people to think of him as the Great Physician. Seeing him as our doctor means we must also view ourselves as patients.

Since I was introduced to this concept, I have had the privilege of working with doctors and medical students for more than ten years. I have talked with them in their offices and homes, walked beside them through hospital corridors, and observed them in surgery and during hospital rounds. We have discussed the patient-doctor relationship and compared it to our relationship with God. As they embraced the parallels I presented and used them in conversations with their patients, they added many details and nuances that I had not previously seen. One doctor in particular, David Schiedermayer of the Medical College of Wisconsin, believed strongly enough in the fitness of this analogy that he encouraged me to write it down so others would also have access to it.

Many friends and colleagues have since shared in the process, but none more faithfully than my wife, Maja. Even though she has heard me teach these ideas for years, she read the manuscript as an "average reader." She often lovingly reminded me to "keep it simple" and sent me back to the keyboard.

Maja's unique contribution to this work parallels that of the analogy itself. I needed the help she was able to give, but that's not all the help I needed. Even though we need the contribution the doctor-patient analogy can bring to our faith, we need what other analogies can add as well. So, as you read, I encourage you to keep all this in perspective. And remember that all analogies break down at some point. This one does, too. Although most of what is ideal in a doctor-patient relationship is true for the God-person relationship, there is at least one major difference between the human model and the heavenly one. The human doctor does not seek our fellowship *after* the professional relationship ends—but the Great Physician heals us precisely so that we can have an ongoing love relationship with him.

One last note: After each of the chapters, you will find a series of questions and some space to fill in the answers. The questions are intended to help you think beyond the material you have just read, and there is space for answers so you will be more encouraged to write down your thoughts. Writing helps you crystallize your thinking. If you write down your answers, you will get more out of the process now, and later be able to return and think more along the same lines.

1

Why We Need a Doctor

"I have seen his ways, but I will heal him.
I will lead him and restore comfort to him and to
    his mourners,
Creating the praise of the lips.
Peace, peace to him who is far and to him who is
    near,"
Says the Lord, "and I will heal him" (Isa. 57:18–19).

In a corner of the emergency room a disheveled woman wept bitterly because her husband of five years lay dead on the gurney behind the curtain. The doctors had been unable to save him. "We didn't know he had a bad heart!" she explained. "We just didn't know! He was young and seemed so strong and full of life. We'd just come from a party with friends when he collapsed in the kitchen. If only we'd known. . . ."

Across the room another anguished voice began, "He'd seen it on the TV. You know, how someone could cut himself open to get the bullet out after being shot. He told me he could do it. He's my older brother. He could do *anything!*—Only, this time he couldn't."

We need God to be our doctor because in our sinful condition we are like those two dead men in the emergency room. We have defective hearts and we cannot save ourselves.

Luke 5:27–32 tells of Levi the tax-gatherer, sitting in his shack at work for the Roman government, collecting as much money as he could extort from the local populace. He knew the religious leaders considered him a sinner, which kept him out of their circle of friends. But Levi had his own friends, and he felt fine. He had no idea that the Lord hates it when we depend on money to provide a good future for ourselves at the expense of other people. Neither did he realize that trusting in his own ability to bring security and stability to his life was an insult to his Creator. However, when Jesus brought his message of God's power to heal both spiritual and physical disease, Levi—known also as Matthew—set aside all he had to follow Jesus when he called him. That night this grateful patient invited all his friends, also sick with the same desperate disease, to meet the doctor who brought healing to his soul. They, too, heard Jesus' message. And they heard his exchange with the Pharisees who had gathered outside the tax-gatherer's "clinic."

When the religious leaders challenged him about associating with "sinners," Jesus responded, "It is not those who are well who need a physician, but those who are sick. I have not come to call the righteous but sinners to repentance" (vv. 31–32). In saying this, he left little doubt that the people at the tax-gatherer's party needed his intervention as much as physically diseased people need the healing expertise of a medical doctor. We need the Lord to diagnose our problem; we need him to prescribe and effect the cure; and we need him to guide us along the road to recovery.

The Need for Diagnosis

Because sin is always fatal, we need to have our spiritual illness diagnosed. Every physical disease, left to itself, runs a natural course. If it is diagnosed accurately and quickly, even the most deadly diseases can usually be controlled if not cured. The most dangerous illnesses are those that mask their destructive power. Sin is like the worst of these. If we do not find out that our imperfect hearts are corrupting every part of our lives, we will succumb to spiritual death.

The Great Physician offers us a sobering picture of what ails us: Every human being is born with terminal "heart disease." Our hearts, the faculty of the soul where our affections dwell, our plans are evaluated, and our commitments are made, cause us to live under the dreadful prospect of the wrath of God. Instead of bringing forth delight in God and love for him and for other people, the unregenerate, unhealed human heart produces arrogance toward God, insincere worship, and "evil thoughts, fornications, thefts, murders, adulteries, deeds of coveting and wickedness, as well as deceit, sensuality, envy, slander, pride and foolishness" (Mark 7:21–22). Apart from God's intervention, we tend to continue in the same style of life, going from bad to worse, deceiving and being deceived, because our hearts are incurably wicked. We are our own worst enemies and we don't even know it!

Although we need this diagnosis before healing can begin, knowledge alone is not enough. Modern doctors know from experience that even when people are told that they have a life-threatening illness, they often deny it. Because they refuse to recognize the dangerous condition of their bodies and submit to the necessary treatment, they die. Likewise, the Bible is filled with stories of people who refused to accept God's diagnosis of their spiritual condition. Jesus, referring to a prophecy of Isaiah, said, "The heart of this people has become dull, and they scarcely hear with their ears. And they have closed their eyes, lest they should see with their eyes and understand with their heart and repent, so that I may heal them" (Matt. 13:15 DWK).

THE NEED FOR A CURE

Denial of the Lord's diagnosis is one of the symptoms of having spiritual heart disease, and it indicates the severity of our problem. Having a sinful heart is dangerous in that we cannot cure ourselves. The apostle Paul agreed with Jesus' assessment of our condition and adds: "the mind [heart] set on the flesh is death, but the mind set on the Spirit is life and peace, because the mind set on the flesh is hostile toward God; for it does not subject itself to the law of God, for it is not even able to do so" (Rom. 8:6–7).

Just as Jeremiah relates the words of the Lord that our hearts are incurably sick and impossible to diagnose on our own, Paul says that we are "not even able to" subject ourselves to God's Law. Does this inability mean that we are not held responsible for the decisions we make to rebel against the Great Physician's orders to trust his counsel on how to live a healthy, happy life? No, it does not! For this inability is due not to a physical inadequacy but to foolhardy moral choices.

When my optometrist gave me my contact lenses for the first time, he showed me how to blink properly, so that the surface of my eyes would be properly lubricated. Then he told me to walk around for an hour while practicing this blinking pattern, so I would develop the habit of blinking this new way. If my eyelids had been sewn to the upper and lower portions of my eye sockets, I would not have been held *morally* responsible for following his instructions. Since my eyelids were free, however, the only "inability" that could prevent me from obeying would be my desire to do something else. I would be held morally responsible for disobedience in this case, because I was physically able to comply. The only reason for not obeying would be my desire not to obey. Moral inability is simply having so strong a desire for "something else" that we choose it rather than any other option.

Since Adam and Eve's disobedience, we human beings have passed on the inclination to choose what brings glory to ourselves and to turn away from choices that yield praise to God. The knowledge of God is readily available through the universe around us, but we foolishly choose to look to the creation rather than to the Creator for our joy. And even when we do try to respond to God's commands, we intend to boast in what *we* have accomplished. We have pursued the law of righteousness—not through faith, but as though by "works" (see Rom. 9:31–32). In other words, we behaved as the Lord commanded, but not because of our joyful confidence in his ability to do great and mighty things for us. Instead, we obeyed because of our desire to feel as though we were self-sufficient, independent, and contributing citizens rather than recipients of charity. This is just another way of worshiping the creature rather than the Creator.

If the heart that desires to glorify itself rather than its Creator is not replaced, we face the prospect of suffering God's righteous anger for eternity. And we could only look forward to an anxious, frustrating existence before our death on earth. Without the security and stability of an eternal source of goodness, humans in a self-deceived, self-exalting state can only hope in their own ability to satisfy the deep thirsts and hungers of their souls. Without the promise of eternal joy provided by a divine being who is infinitely more wise and powerful than we are, humans must settle for all the temporary joy we can wrest from the environment and the people around us.

God furnishes a cure-all by giving us new hearts. He sees us in our desperate state and provides the remedy we can't even admit we need.

> "Moreover, I will give you a new heart and put a new spirit within you; and I will remove the heart of stone from your flesh and give you a heart of flesh" (Ezek. 36:26).

> ". . . I will be their God; and I will give them one heart and one way, that they may fear Me always, for their own good" (Jer. 32:38–39).

THE NEED FOR THERAPY

As with some physical diseases, the cure for sin only begins with surgery. Therapy and strengthening of our "new heart" must complete the process. We must pursue the sanctification that will enable us to live free of further infection. We might be tempted to think that just because the old heart is gone, we will never again desire anything that is contrary to God's design for our lives, and therefore will not need to continue in the Divine Doctor's care. Not so! In some strange way and in the wisdom of our surgeon, pockets of infection (desires for self-glorification) still remain in our souls. Although with the new heart we receive God's Spirit, which in a way reestablishes our spiritual immune system, now an inner battle will rage between our sin-filled flesh and the new heart that God has given us.

Paul accurately describes this battle:

I joyfully concur with the principle of God that is in my heart, but I see a different principle in the members of my body, waging war against the principle in my heart, and making me a prisoner of the principle of sin which is in my members. . . . On the one hand, with my heart I am serving the principle of God, but on the other, with my flesh the principle of sin (Rom. 7:22–25 DWK).

So we find that there is a constant need to continue to see the Great Physician—to be reminded of his prescription for our health, to be encouraged to follow his guidelines, and to be treated for our setbacks—as we are motivated by the picture of perfect health and its benefits, which our spiritual doctor holds out to us.

When God in his mercy and grace comes to us and removes "the heart of stone" and replaces it with a Spirit-filled "heart of flesh," we experience the miracle of new birth. It is as though a wise and caring doctor, on his way home from the hospital, finds us lying on the sidewalk in cardiac arrest. God lifts us up, carries us to his hospital, performs the surgical operation, transfuses us with the blood of his Son, and breathes life back into us by means of his Holy Spirit. There is also awakened in us a new view of God and his creation by means of the presentation of his words in Scripture. He then places us in the convalescent home called "the church" and begins to teach us how to live in such a way that we grow strong and healthy and free from the fear of ever dying a spiritual death again. We become outpatients in his clinic of rehabilitative medicine and look forward to his being our personal, primary-care doctor for eternity:

God, being rich in mercy, because of his great love with which he loved us, even when we were dead in our transgressions, made us alive together in Christ (by grace you have been saved), and raised us up together and seated us together in the heavenlies in Christ Jesus, in order that in the ages to come he might show us the surpassing riches of his grace in Christ Jesus in kindness to us (Eph. 2:4–7 DWK).

This heart-transplant operation is a once-and-for-all event, but rehabilitation requires a lifetime. In the chapters that follow we will consider more thoroughly what it means to live as patients under the loving care of the Great Physician.

For *Reflection*

1. How would you summarize this chapter's explanation of why we need the Great Physician to some junior-highers—in *their* terms?

2. What was your emotional response to the Scripture references that indicate our complete self-centeredness?

3. What was your first indication that your "heart
   transplant" had occurred? What pockets of infection (desire for self-glorification) do you encounter
   most frequently now?

2

God in the Doctor's Role

Jesus . . . said to her, "Everyone who drinks of this water shall thirst again; but whoever drinks of the water that I shall give him shall never thirst; but the water that I shall give him shall become in him a well of water springing up to eternal life" (John 4:13–14).

"I am the bread of life; he who comes to Me shall not hunger, and he who believes in Me shall never thirst" (John 6:35).

In February 1990, *Washington Post Health* published an article entitled: "The Question Your Doctor Doesn't Ask: Are You Satisfied?" The idea here was that a doctor must be concerned about more than simply defeating a disease process. The mental and emotional state of the patient must occupy a physician's thoughts as well, because physical illness affects more than just the body. The relationship between doctor and patient requires that they connect at more than just one level of existence. A good doctor won't be content if his or her patient is dissatisfied. So doctors must examine not only how well they apply their medical skills, but also how well they incorporate who they are as a person into what they do. If this is true for doctors—and I believe it is—how much more will it be true for the Great Physician?

THE GOD WHO WORKS

One way a doctor can satisfy patients is by convincing the patients that the doctor is working for their benefit, not using them for personal gain (whether to bolster his or her ego or reputation or worldly goods). An important feature of the doctor's relationship with the patient is providing a service that the patient cannot supply. If the analogy of viewing God as our doctor is to hold true, should we not be able to think of God as the "worker" in our relationship, as someone who serves on *our* behalf? The prophet Isaiah says: "From of old no one has heard nor perceived by ear, neither has the eye seen a God besides you, who works in behalf of the one who waits for him" (Isa. 64:4).

The Lord God has declared this positively, by affirming that he alone works on behalf of his people. He also defines the relationship by stating just as clearly that any who would relate to him rightly must see him this way. He is totally self-sufficient, having no void or lack that a human can fulfill (see Ps. 50:14–15; Acts 17:24–25).

Does emphasizing this aspect of the Divine Doctor's relationship to us degrade him? Does it reduce him to the role of a cosmic bellboy? No! On the contrary, it exalts him. No part of this picture places *us* in a position of superiority. Every part of it places us in the humbling posture of admitting our inability to help ourselves. As supplicants of grace and mercy, we can do nothing to obligate the Creator—owner and sustainer of the universe—to act on our behalf. We cannot bribe him. We cannot coerce him. We cannot blackmail him. We can only go to him and wait until he is gracious to us. We can only place our future in his hands, submitting ourselves to his wisdom and his timing for the good that he has promised to do in our lives.

An orthopedist is not degraded when a patient comes and asks him or her to set a broken leg. An oncologist is not dishonored when someone asks for the expertise that will rid him of the cancers on his face. A dentist is not debased when a young boy submits himself for repair of the cavities in his teeth. Neither is God degraded, dishonored, or debased when we come to him for whatever needs we have. Anyone who offers a service or a benefit should be delighted to be sought out to render that service!

No other god is like *our* God, who with boundless grace works for those who wait for him. All the other entities from whom we might seek a happy future require that we serve *their* needs. Money, power, sex, reputation, or specific "deities" such as Baal, Thor, or Krishna, require our efforts on their behalf if we are to obtain the benefits we desire from them. For example, if we place our hope for a secure and stable future on money, we can't just announce our desire to a bag of gold in a Fort Knox vault. To obtain the benefits money affords we must expend great effort to build or acquire a sufficient amount of it to do us any good. We must also exercise great wisdom in how we allocate the buying power that it has, so that we don't run out. Likewise, we must carefully safeguard it, for it cannot secure itself from deterioration or theft. In the end, because we must find a way to escape from the great dissatisfaction we feel with money's *inability* to meet our needs fully, despair can be the only final certainty.

The Lord calls upon his infinite skills and wisdom and strength when he works for us. This doctor puts his reputation on the line when he encourages us to seek only him to heal us from the disease of sin in a way satisfying to both the patient and himself.

CHARACTERISTICS OF THE WORKER-DOCTOR

I have asked physicians and dentists and students in those fields what they consider to be some of the most important characteristics needed in a good doctor. Not surprisingly, the same characteristics mentioned by the professionals have appeared on surveys done in a variety of patient populations as well. Even less surprising is how closely these characteristics describe the Lord in his working relationship with us.

Compassionate Love

All people have a strong need to feel loved. We need to sense that someone with whom we have a relationship values us and will act in accord with that decision. Doctors need to be loving and to demonstrate this affection by their use of compassion. The God who is working as our Great Physician loves us and is moved by our condition. "Just as a father tenderly loves his children, so the Lord tenderly loves those who fear him. For he himself knows our frame. He knows well that we are dust" (Ps. 103:13–14 DWK).

The Lord knows our constitution, our essential being, recognizing that we are finite and frail and weak and corruptible. He knows this because he created us. He knows it because he came and lived on earth as one of us.

The English word *compassion* literally means "to feel with." It indicates our being so touched by the plight of someone else, that we are moved to render assistance of some kind. This is exactly the way the Great Physician operates. We are never just an interesting case on which he can show off his skills. Rather, he demonstrates his expertise by patiently working to bring healing to those whom he has chosen to love. He has sovereignly decided to see his patients as *valuable*. The affection that arises in his heart because of this decision is what we call "love." The actions that issue forth for the benefit of his patients are also what we call "love." We are created to respond positively to those who show us how much they value us by their initiatives and by their sensitive responses to our desperate circumstances. So we expect our doctors to be compassionately loving in their relationship with us. And this is always what we see in the way God treats us— with mercy and love (see Eph. 2:4).

Commitment

We also want someone to work for us who will be committed to our care for the duration of the process. We would get extremely angry if a doctor gave up in the middle of the treatment. I know a family whose daughter had severe scoliosis at birth. Several physicians treated her until the parents were no longer able to pay and then informed the family that they could do nothing more for the girl. They finally found a doctor who *committed* himself to care for their daughter until there was no longer a need. He put everything he had as a doctor on the line for this family—his expertise and his reputation.

The kind of commitment we desire of a doctor has two faces. Doctors must be committed to their own glory as well as being committed to *our* good. These are not contradictory motives, nor are they detrimental to the doctor-patient relationship. On the contrary, they are both necessary to the success of the rehabilitation efforts. If doctors are not concerned about their name—how they are perceived by those who look at their work—they will not be motivated to do their very best nor to expend every effort on behalf of their patients. However, this alone will not guarantee a doctor's best effort. He or she must also be dedicated to the good of every patient. This commitment helps prevent a doctor from using patients to create a false image on his or her own behalf. It both narrows the behavioral choices of the clinician and works to maintain a love for the patient. It is impossible to hate or to be indifferent to those for whom one is committed to doing good.

We see both of these commitments in God, the Great Physician. He is committed to his own glory when he says through Ezekiel, "I will vindicate the holiness of My great name which has been profaned among the nations, which you have profaned in their midst. Then the nations will know that I am the LORD, when I prove Myself holy among you in their sight" (Ezek. 36:23). We know this is true. And Jesus underscores this commitment when he asks the Father to glorify the two of them with the glory they had before creation (John 17:1, 5).

God is also committed to our welfare and our joy. He promises us a future in which we will never weep, because there will be no one who will harm his people. He even tells us that his most difficult commands are designed to fill us with joy (see Isaiah 65 and John 15).

We willingly place ourselves in the hands of doctors who delight in doing us good, whose pleasure it is to extend themselves for us. How much more ought we to entrust our recovery from sin to the Great Physician whose pleasure it is to reconcile us to himself and pour his blessings on us forever. God is most glorified in us when we are most satisfied in him.

Competence

It is not enough for doctors to be compassionate and committed to our care if they are not competent. In the minds of some, this quality ought to be listed first, for many patients have tolerated an absence of compassion and/or commitment simply because their doctor is extremely skilled. But that is an accommodation to the imperfection of the current health-care system. On the other hand, other people will put up with a lack of competence if compassion and commitment are evident in the doctor-patient relationship.

In the battle to overcome the effects of sin in our lives, competence is a critical factor for inspiring faithful obedience. When the stakes are high and the outcome so important, we cannot afford to risk following the advice of someone who doesn't know what he or she is doing. In the realm of physical healing, we only care if the doctor is competent in a particular field of medicine (or dentistry). A doctor doesn't have to be omni-competent in every specialty to be regarded as qualified to treat us, nor does competence in unrelated areas guarantee competence in the healing arts.

When we evaluate God, who promises to rid us of our inclination to insult his glory, we need to know that he is competent to work the necessary changes in us. For us to be able to trust our recovery to God, we must see that he is able both to rid us of sin and to govern the universe perfectly. And he *does* govern perfectly. His resting on the "seventh day" of creation implies that everything he had done up to that time was exactly the way he wanted it. We never see God running around fixing things that have gone awry. Because the universe was made correctly the first time, we should infer his total competence in how he operates.

In the Book of Job (chaps. 38–41), God declares the breadth and depth of his wisdom and power in the governing of his creation. The Lord uses a series of questions designed to enable Job to own up to his finitude and ineptitude in the mundane details of everyday existence and with regard to God's efforts to maintain the moral balance of creation. God asks Job, "Can you send forth lightnings that they may go and say to you, 'Here we are'? Who has put wisdom in the innermost being or given understanding to the mind?" (38:35–36). And he challenges Job to clothe himself "with honor and majesty" and to "look on everyone who is proud and humble him" and "tread down the wicked" (40:10–12). At the conclusion of this litany, Job replies with the only reasonable answer: "I know that you can" do all things, and that no purpose of God's will be impeded (42:2 DWK).

God's absolute competence is also seen in his ability to keep from being contaminated by his dealings with our sin. Competent human doctors do not become victims of "iatrogenesis," a related infection acquired during treatment of a patient. Neither does the Great Physician. He always acts so that his love for his glory is clear. No one could ever charge him with being unrighteous when he rids us of our sinful ways.

The beginning of the story of Job shows this principle at work. Satan challenges the way God deals with Job, saying that Job only worships God because God has bribed him with many possessions and other blessings. What befalls Job after that is intended by God to prove this charge false. Job's immediate response of faith in the face of loss shows that Job loves God because of the goodness of God displayed in the gifts. God justifies himself before charges of wrongdoing and maintains himself as worthy of all worship.

The Lord again faces the charge of being "unrighteous" when he begins to forgive sinners on a large scale at the conclusion of Jesus' earthly ministry. How can the righteous, holy God separate sin from the sinner—"as far as the east is from the west" (Ps. 103:12)—so that he is true to his love for the glory of his goodness, which sinners have scorned? He can't just sweep sin under the rug as if it were nothing! Doing that would imply that our rejection of him in favor of self-worship is not such a heinous crime. So he demonstrates his infinite, unexcelled, and irreplaceable worth through the life, death, resurrection, and ascension of the incarnate second person of the Godhead (see Rom. 3:24–26).

The incarnation is the surgical ensemble that God wears when he opens our hearts to remove our sin and cast it into oblivion. Just as we would not entrust our care to a surgeon foolish enough to operate on an AIDS patient without protection, neither should we trust a god who is not competent enough to remove our sin without becoming sinful himself. Is God that competent? Yes, the resurrection proves it. We can entrust ourselves totally to him "who raised Jesus our Lord from the dead, He who was delivered up because of our transgressions, and was raised because of our justification" (Rom. 4:24–25).

Availability

In times past, before the proliferation of specialties in the health-care arena, the general practitioner was the norm. Each professional was called on to provide all the medical or dental care his or her patients needed. One of the characteristics valued by everyone was the ready availability of the care-giver. The average doctor was on call twenty-four hours a day, seven days a week—at home, at church, at the office, about town. Even today, ready access is valued in primary-care practitioners.

This is not just a matter of emotional support for sick patients or the worried well. If the doctor is not readily available, proper and timely care cannot be given. The long lines at many hospital emergency rooms attest to the fact that not enough doctors are on hand to meet immediate needs, either at their offices or the hospital, or in the community. Since even fully trained nurses are not allowed to make certain medical decisions and must first consult with a doctor, proper health management demands that a physician be within reach when needed.

When our doctor is God, we have a care-giver who is *always* available. We have someone who understands our problems as we recover from our sin and who is instantly ready to help in time of trouble. The Divine Doctor walks with us every moment of every day. He knows our voice and our "medical history," so he never confuses us with anyone else when we call for help. No appointment is necessary, for he delights to work for us, day or night. He is ready and willing and eager to display his glory by taking care of us in just the right way, at just the right time. "The righteous cry and the LORD hears, And delivers them out of all their troubles. The LORD is near to the brokenhearted, And saves those who are crushed in spirit" (Ps. 34:17–18).

The Bible is full of assurances that God, who works on our behalf to rid us of the effects and power of sin, is near and ready to meet us in our moments of need. He knows our need, so we ought to be honest with him. He knows what will help, so we ought to call on him for the assistance he offers. He knows the right moment to act, so we ought to be patient as we await his efforts. "And we know that God causes all things to work together for good to those who love God, to those who are called according to His purpose" (Rom. 8:28).

Teaching Skills

The word *doctor* originally denoted a teacher. It comes from the same root from which we derive the word *doc-*

trine. One of the primary characteristics necessary to a facilitator of healing is the ability to teach. Doctors must be able to communicate accurately and emphatically the necessary information concerning our condition and their rehabilitation plan.

In the world of physical healing, we want to be able to ask the doctor questions and hear his answers firsthand. We want to interact face to face with the care-giver and to receive instructions that are clear and within the scope of our comprehension. We want to know what are our chances for full recovery and what will happen to us during the treatment period. We want to know how to avoid the dangers and pitfalls along the way. We expect the doctor to have the information. We expect the doctor to teach us in terms we can understand. Clearly, the better the communicator, the better the outcome.

Just as this is one of the characteristics we look for in any doctor who is treating us physically, so we find it in the Great Physician in full measure. He often uses unusual techniques to enhance our knowledge base, to enlighten our understanding, and to encourage our thoughtful consideration. What he has to communicate is not always what we want to hear, because it often requires that we completely restructure either our perception of reality or our pattern of response or both. But he *is* our teacher, and the instruction he gives us in Scripture is designed to make our recovery as delightful as possible. We experience his teaching as we walk along the paths of life and reflect on his promise: "I will instruct you and teach you in the way which you should go; I will counsel you with My eye upon you" (Ps. 32:8; cf. Ps. 25:8–9; Phil. 4:13; 2 Tim. 3:16–17).

Intimately Knowledgeable

Good doctors know their patients as individuals, not just as a collection of medical data or examples of human anatomy. It is not always simple for them to know us this way. One of the struggles confronting today's professionals in medicine and dentistry is how best to join modern science with the *art* of healing. Orientation during years of undergraduate study is mainly scientific. This means that enormous amounts of energy are spent learning about the systems of the human body and developing skills for keeping them functioning properly. The first two years of graduate studies are designed to strengthen this knowledge and these skills. When exposed to clinical diagnostic procedures, students discover that there is still more to treating sick people. Skills are developed that help doctors understand and treat the whole *person* rather than the symptoms of a particular ailment.

When students spend time with both pretend and real patients under the supervision of experienced clinicians, in almost all of these controlled encounters the students stand in the position of healer. They appear strong and educated and whole in the presence of the weak and disabled and learn to ask questions and observe behaviors. Young doctors are taught to be objective and "unemotional" so that they can provide the best possible therapy. But there is one problem when objectivity is used as the sole approach to medical education: Striving for it tends to lead to relating to people as objects.

To overcome this obstacle to sound treatment, good doctors build up a bank of personal information about us. Their knowledge of us as individuals fosters a sense of predictability in our personal interactions. It facilitates the creation of trust because it enables a more effective communication process, and it therefore helps focus the clinical reasoning behind medical, ethical, and patient-care decisions.

The Great Physician knows us intimately. Scripture affirms that he guided our formation in our mother's wombs and can number the very hairs on our heads. He knows our sleeping habits and the patterns of our activities. According to David, all our days were "written" in his book before we even existed (Ps. 139:16). Even with five billion individuals on earth, the Lord does not confuse any one of us with any other person. His bank of personal information on each of us is full of all the intimate details of our lives, including our thoughts, attitudes, emotions, and motives. Nothing escapes his notice.

God knows us in another way as well. Some doctors gain insight into the doctor-patient relationship by becoming patients themselves. Sometimes, when this happens, an account of the experience is published so other doctors can learn from it vicariously. Their idea is not new. The Triune God used this tactic long ago. The Father sent his Son Jesus to be one of us because it was even more meaningful for the one who was to save us to suffer in the same way his patients suffer. The Savior would share our humanity so that his death would "render powerless him who had the power of death, that is, the devil; and might deliver those who through fear of death were subject to slavery all their lives" (Heb. 2:14–15). Since we have someone who can empathize totally with our weaknesses—who has been tempted in the same ways we are tempted, *but without sinning*—we can, and should, go to him so we "may receive mercy and find grace to help in time of need" (Heb. 4:16).

SATISFIED AND RELATED

We could list other characteristics that would expand on the exemplary doctor we have briefly examined here. But none of them should detract from a care-giver's ability to provide the satisfaction we desire in both the outcome and the relationship. Some might argue that human doctors cannot get intimately involved with every patient. Although this may be true, every patient wants to feel that a mutually satisfying relationship exists in some form. Often, much of the credit for a good outcome medically has as much to do with the doctor-patient relationship as with the medical protocol.

On the spiritual plane, a somewhat different outcome is in view. We aim at recovery from the effects and power of sin precisely *so that* we can enjoy an ongoing relationship with our divine healer. Here the characteristics of the doctor become even more critical to the process. And it is on this plane that we can rejoice to see that no characteristic of a "good doctor" is lacking in the Great Physician.

For *Reflection*

1. Describe two recent instances in which God has *worked* for you. What made it clear that God was at work?

2. Pretend you are having a conversation with a neighbor. How would you make clear why it's so important for God to be the *worker* in our relationship with him?

3. Besides the ones cited, what other passages of Scripture teach us that our desire for happiness and God's desire to be glorified are complementary and therefore succeed together?

4. What other characteristics of a "good doctor" besides the ones mentioned does Jesus demonstrate? (List the Scripture passages that substantiate these.)

3

More Than We Expect

"I am the true vine, and My Father is the vine-dresser. Every branch in Me that does not bear fruit, He takes away; and every branch that bears fruit, He prunes it, that it may bear more fruit" (John 15:1–2).

When my wife taught in public school, she once met one of her third-grade students in the grocery store. The student was incredulous. He couldn't believe that his teacher was there—where "normal" people shopped. She asked why he was so surprised. He answered that he thought she lived at the school.

Most of us would chuckle at that story, and few of us think our doctors spend all their lives in their offices or at the hospital (unless we ask a doctor's spouse). Yet I can remember not long ago being quite surprised to see my dentist at a shopping mall.

The doctor-patient relationship is essentially a professional alliance. The doctor professes to work for our good, and we agree to be the clients for whom he or she works. The relationship has certain boundaries and rules by which we as patients learn to know our doctors and they us. We rarely become close friends, yet we want to have open communication with these amazing people who care so intimately for us. We want to be able to anticipate what they will do, to predict the trajectory of our paths together. We want the security of familiarity and understanding, but we also want to believe that *we* are in control of what they will do with our lives. We want to keep them in their boxes so we can make them available to us on demand—and then only to do what we want them to do and all that we want them to do.

The previous chapter showed how ideally suited God is to be our Great Physician. Yet we must remember that when we call any doctor to be involved in our care, we cannot remain in complete control. We relinquish the authority to determine what is best for us. It is *because* we don't know what to do that we seek someone with more qualifications to help us. But we often forget that the doctor may have something in mind for us that is quite different from what we anticipated! There is unpredictability in the sovereignty a healer exercises for our good.

The doctor-patient relationship is somewhat one-sided in that the patient does not control what doctors prescribe. Rather, as patients we must be ready for "surprises" in the one to whom we have entrusted our lives. This does not mean that doctors will be capricious or whimsical, but we must be prepared for them to expand our idea of what healers are and how they operate. A good doctor will be compassionate, committed, competent, available, and informative—but may exhibit these traits in ways we might not anticipate or like.

To the extent that we are prepared for new and different approaches by our doctor, we will benefit from his or her knowledge, skill, and compassion. If we demand that doctors always operate in one way, if we insist that we control how they handle our case, we forfeit or truncate the experience of the good that they can do for us while we are under their care. Good doctors will come when we call, make all their medical knowledge available when we need it, and will want us to return to health, bringing all their energy to bear on our behalf. But we need to be ready to step beyond the boundaries of what we might consider comfortable and appropriate if we are to receive the benefits that such expertise offers.

When I went to see my orthopedist after my back surgery, he really shocked me. He told me I would have to begin to exercise! Worse, he told me I would have to bring myself to the point of pain before it would do any good. Worst, he said that if I worked so that I caused too much pain, I would set myself back. This assignment was not what I wanted to hear. He had been so tender in his care. Now he was being tough. Pain during rehabilitation had not been part of the recovery model I had imagined. So I had to adjust my expectations. I learned that the doctor was multi-dimensional in his relationship to me and my healing, and that I was not the one ultimately in control of it.

We have already examined some of the characteristics of the Great Physician that are analogous to those of human doctors, so it is probably obvious how readily we should go to the Lord to be healed from the disease of sin. For the rest of this chapter I want to focus on some of the "surprises" we will experience as we get to know the Great Physician and his ministrations in our lives. His unpredictability will not lessen our affection for him, but rather draw us closer to him.

Gentle but Not Tame

When we suffer injury or disease, we want our doctor to be gentle with us. The malady is bad enough, so we want to avoid any severe discomfort in our treatment. But because doctors are committed to our health, they often must ask us, in their most sensitive way, to adopt totally new lifestyles or to follow rigorous, daunting regimens. Although it is often with reluctance that we follow such orders, time usually proves them correct. Our health improves and our affection for the care-giver increases when the doctor is "gentle but not tame."

The same is true of the Great Physician. He is sympathetic but never subdued! He promises benefits that we can hardly comprehend, but he asks us to take risks in the context of our confidence in him. He tells us to find our satisfaction in him alone. We can't look for this in our families, our surroundings, or even in our own physical well-being. Jesus said, "Whoever does not carry his own cross and come after Me cannot be my disciple" (Luke 14:27). He promises "houses and lands and brothers and sisters and mothers in this life in the fellowship of his followers, and eternal life with all its blessings in the age to come" (Mark 10:30 DWK). But in the same sentence he promises "persecutions." We sing in the old hymn, "There is a wideness in God's mercy." We ought also to sing, "There is a *wildness* in God's mercy." Living by faith in the Divine Doctor is to be radically out of control while in his care.

Philip was an earnest young believer who came to Christ shortly after the resurrection and ascension. The body of believers in Jerusalem noted that he was one of seven who could be described as "full of the Spirit and wisdom." So they chose him as one of the first deacons. Not long after this, he went down to Samaria because of some of the persecution Jesus had predicted. There, as

Philip aided in the process of spiritual transplantation and recovery, he demonstrated the amazing power of the Divine Doctor to release a person from the effects of sin. But he was not allowed to settle down in that city. Instead, the Lord instructed him to head south into the desert on some unstated mission. On the way he encountered a caravan proceeding home to Ethiopia from Jerusalem. The Lord said, "Go up and join the lead chariot." When Philip obeyed, he found one of the leading officials of Ethiopia searching to understand Isaiah 53. Philip explained so clearly and convincingly that this passage referred to Jesus as the coming sin-bearer that the Ethiopian proclaimed his submission and allegiance to the Great Physician. Then Philip was "snatched away" by the "Spirit of the Lord" and found himself in a city miles away. Did God take him through this wild experience only for the benefit of the Ethiopian? No, it was also for Philip's enlightenment, for he continued to preach the gospel wherever he went. (See Acts 8:5–40.)

Centuries earlier, after the prophet Elijah had seen the Lord bring about the downfall of the prophets of Baal, he went into hiding in the wilderness, for he feared for his life. He was so afraid of the pagan Queen Jezebel's revenge that he even asked the Lord to *take* his life. But the Great Physician commanded Elijah to meet with him at Horeb, the mountain of God. When he arrived, Elijah experienced several exotic events, each one of which might have been considered evidence of the presence of the one to whom he had entrusted his life. But the Divine Doctor was not in the whirlwind, the earthquake, or the fire. That was how Elijah wanted him to appear and work: dramatically, cataclysmically, devastatingly. But the Lord is gentle but not tame! He would not work according to Elijah's demands. Rather, he announced his presence with a gentle breeze. His actions were under *his* control, not Elijah's. So also was the condition of the rest of his

7,000 patients, the children of Israel of whom Elijah was unaware. When Elijah humbled himself and approached the Divine Doctor to hear how he would handle his case, he learned a few details of how God would handle all the situations Elijah feared, but not necessarily the way Elijah had expected, for he was removing Elijah from the scene. *A good doctor is gentle but not tame.*

STRONG BUT NOT COOPERATIVE

One sensation we experience when we are sick is that everything seems to be out of control. The more serious the disease, the greater this sensation. It is not a feeling we enjoy experiencing. None of us functions very well in a state of insecurity. We must know that either we, or someone we trust, is in control, and an illness makes it look as though the very opposite is true. So we go to a doctor because we view that person as someone who can help us regain mastery of our life. But to our surprise, the doctor doesn't give us control; instead, he or she takes charge! A good doctor is strong but not cooperative with our agendas. So, too, the Great Physician is able to arrange or to do anything he desires, but his wisdom and purpose guide the application of this ability. Therefore, although we see from our point of view that with our minds we may plan our ways, the Lord directs our steps (Prov. 16:9). The Scriptures are filled with statements like the one he makes in Isaiah 46:9–11:

> "Remember the former things long past,
> For I am God, and there is no other;
> I am God, and there is no one like Me,
> Declaring the end from the beginning
> And from ancient times things which have not been done,
> Saying, 'My purpose will be established,
> And I will accomplish all My good pleasure.'"

God will bring about *his* purpose in *his* way, according to *his* plan, so that *he* is the one who receives praise. As we saw earlier, the Great Physician is committed to accomplish our good in a way that highlights the glory of the goodness he has to offer. This means we must let him decide our treatment plan. I know of few things that irritate a doctor more than being told by patients what treatment plan they believe they should follow. Such an attitude on a patient's part is really an insult to the doctor. It suggests that he or she cannot be trusted to know what is best for the patient or cannot be depended on to provide the correct therapy when it is needed.

A classic case of trying to get the Great Physician to cooperate with a patient's agenda is found in the Book of Job. (The Bible has several other incidents like this, but none as well developed. We could also cite David's desire to build the temple; Paul's urge to preach the Gospel in Asia Minor; Jesus' wish to avoid the cross.) In the previous chapter we considered part of Job's story and learned something about the competence of the Great Physician. To maintain his reputation as worthy of our total worship and trust, he allowed a limited attack upon Job by forces intent on Job's destruction. The extent of the damage was controlled, and the intent of the Divine Doctor was to elicit Job's continued confidence in God's ability to provide the best of care in every situation.

To make matters even more confusing, especially for the patient, the Great Physician decided to use Job's situation for another purpose. Even after Job proved the righteousness of God by maintaining his faith in the midst of suffering, the Lord did not restore him to his former state. Rather, he allowed the effects of Satan's attacks to linger. Job's obvious agenda was to obtain immediate relief from his pain. And his doctor obviously had the know-how and power to provide such relief, but he did not cooperate with Job's plan of treatment.

As Job's problems continued unabated, this long-suffering man began to question the wisdom and righteousness of the very doctor to whom he had committed his care. He viewed his treatment as capricious and unjustified. In the end he heard from his friend Elihu that the Lord had a different plan, that he wanted Job to be purified from his religious pride, a condition that Job didn't realize he had and that would not have surfaced in any other way. Then the Divine Doctor addressed Job directly. Between Elihu's and God's arguments, Job finally realized that God's power to do him good was really at work, although not according to Job's agenda. When Job repented of his arrogance, God stopped the unpleasant but cleansing procedure, pronounced it a success, and brought Job back to his normally happy state. *A good doctor is strong but not cooperative.*

TENDER BUT NOT SOOTHING

One of the most difficult times in a doctor's life occurs when he must break the news of a painful diagnosis, a poor prognosis, or death. When my mother-in-law died, I was with Papa and my wife in the waiting room. All we knew was that some catastrophic event had occurred while Mama was recovering from a minor injury and that the medical personnel were working as hard as they could to bring her back to consciousness. When her doctor came in, I could see on his face that Mama had not survived. But Papa did not see his face. I stood to greet the doctor, and Papa stood with me. Very gently the doctor tried to tell us that she had died. Papa did not understand. So, in plainer and more direct terms, the doctor delivered his grim message. He put his arm around Papa and began to guide him to where he could see Mama one last time. The doctor was as gentle and tender as he could be, but because he could not deny the fact of her death, he could not soothe away the pain nor alleviate the awfulness of Mama's departure.

The Great Physician, too, has exceptional tenderness, but does not soothe us by downgrading our encounters with bitter reality. Comfort is only possible when pain is openly admitted and acknowledged. We never see the Lord shy away from telling us the truth about our spiritual condition. There are no soothing words of denial for us to misconstrue and use to tell ourselves "rational lies" about how we are really not in such a dangerous situation after all.

Adam and Eve were expelled from the Garden because of their sin. When they left, they understood exactly why they were being evicted. But God was very tender with them in the process. He spoke with them, outlining the nature of the problem and explaining the consequences of their actions. He showed them what they must do for their future and even fashioned protective garments to cover their shame. Nevertheless, he never minced words with them. They were chastised because of their sin— separated from God and doomed to suffering. Yet, because their doctor was tender but not soothing, they were able to face reality, and reestablish the relationship they had broken through their sin.

A similar scene was played out generations later when Jesus interviewed a man who came seeking to obtain the spiritual health offered in Jesus' message. He sensed that something was missing in his life, that his spiritual rating was lower than it should have been. He wanted the secret to "eternal life," so he asked the Divine Doctor to confirm whether or not he was on the right track. Like any good clinician, Jesus asked him some pertinent questions and received seemingly satisfactory answers. Then, in a flash of insight, Jesus saw the problem. This story is told in all three synoptic Gospels, with Matthew describing the man as "young" and Luke characterizing him as "a certain ruler." From the context, we can conclude that this man was not lacking in material wealth. Note the tenderness with which Jesus exposed the petitioner's festering and wounded soul and prescribed a remedy:

> As he looked at him, Jesus loved him and said, "You lack one thing: Go and sell all you possess, and give to the poor, and you shall have treasure in heaven. Then come, follow me" (Mark 10:21 DWK).

This man was so close. He apparently followed the Old Testament law. Couldn't Jesus have just said, "That's really good"? After all, there is no mention in the commandments about not allowing money to be the supreme value in one's life—at least not in so many words. Jesus could have been soothing, but instead, he was bluntly honest. He did not say, as we sometimes do to our children, "Everything will turn out okay." Although he did affirm the good in the man's life, Jesus also exposed the reality of his problem so that he could recognize it and solve it. This troubled patient was invited by Jesus to "follow me," after *first* removing the obstacle that kept him from trusting completely in the Lord. Unfortunately, he rejected the Great Physician's advice: ". . . he went away grieved; for he was one who owned much property" (Matt. 19:22). *A good doctor is tender but not soothing.*

WHAT'S HE LIKE—REALLY?

We know this doctor's credentials. We have heard of his competence and may have already witnessed it. His commitment is evident. His availability is legendary. He cares as no one else ever has or can or will. So we call on him for the goodness he offers. We come to him expecting to experience what we know about him. And we find this. But we find so much more. The Divine Doctor reveals himself in ways we don't anticipate. He forces us to expand our view, to understand him more deeply. There are surprises that we experience because he is sovereign. Putting our faith in the Great Physician means being radically out of control of our future, ultimately conformed to his agenda, yet finally comforted with his healing truth.

For *Reflection*

1. How has the Lord made it clear to you that your life is out of your ultimate control, but well within his?

2. Describe two or three situations in which the Great Physician has surprised you.

3. Describe one or more situations in which the Lord has brought spiritual growth through unusual processes.

4

To Have
and to Hold

All these died in faith, still waiting to receive the promises, but having seen them and welcomed them from a distance, so that they confessed that they were strangers and exiles on earth.... Therefore God is not ashamed to be called their God; for He has prepared a city for them (Hebrews 11:13, 16 DWK).

He who has the Son, has [eternal] life (1 John 5:12).

ittle words can mean a lot. Take the verb *have*. We all think we know what it means. We use it every day. We say, "I have time to read." "Do you have a typewriter?" "Boy, do I have a cold!" "Does your sister have a doctor?" We can discover the essence of the relationship between a doctor and patient by considering this little word *have* and the related concepts found in the words *my, mine* and *your, yours*.

When we speak of relationships between persons, we usually hesitate to use the idea of possession. I do not "have" a daughter in exactly the same sense that I "have" a pencil. I have nearly absolute control over where my pencil is and what it does. I own it and can keep it anywhere I choose. I can use it for writing or abuse it by snapping it between my fingers. It's my pencil. She is my daughter, but I should not (and cannot) exert the same control over her. Nevertheless, there is something similar in having my daughter and having my pencil; and it has to do with influence.

Having means that the connection between me and my possession *allows what I have to influence me according to its nature.* It implies that I must take care to maintain the connection. If I abuse my pencil I will not "have" it for long. If I abuse my daughter, I will still be able to say that I fathered a female child, but she will probably remove herself from the relationship, so that I will not be able to say "I have a daughter." On the other hand, if I act in a gracious way toward her, she will delight in being called *my* daughter. When she relates to me as my daughter, she influences my life in ways only a daughter can. Similarly, when I "have" a cold, it influences me according to its nature. So I do everything I can to disconnect myself from it, so it will no longer exert its power over me.

Doctors *have* patients, and patients *have* doctors. More importantly—but in the same way—gods *have* people and people *have* gods. In the previous two chapters we considered some of the characteristics of the Great Physician. Now we will look at what it means to "have" the Lord as our doctor. For the dynamics of our relationship are informed by this concept. I am his patient and he is my doctor, with the emphasis on *his* and *my.*

The biblical precedent for using this language model begins in Genesis and ends in Revelation. It begins in a promise given to Abram and his seed and ends in its fulfillment. God promised Abram to give him and his seed all the land of Canaan for an everlasting possession and added, "I will be their God" (Gen. 17:1–8). Many generations later, John sees "a new heaven and a new earth," in which he hears a voice saying, "Behold, the tabernacle of God is among men, and He shall dwell among them, and they shall be His people . . ." (Rev. 21:1–3).

From the beginning of this age to the beginning of the age to come, Yahweh the Creator-Redeemer has made it clear that he wants us to "have" him as our God and that he wants to "have" us as his people. This doctor hung out his shingle on the first day and since then has eagerly done all that is necessary to care for the inhabitants of the universe he created.

What does it mean to say that I *have* this personage as *my* God? What does it mean to say that I am *his?* I think it means the same as saying that I *have* this doctor and he *has* me as his patient.

What exactly does it mean to "have" a doctor? According to the previous discussion, it means there is a possessive connection between the doctor and me. The doctor is identified as mine, but this bonding is acknowledged on both sides of the relationship. This further implies that the doctor is obligated to be "for" me. That is, all that he or she is as a doctor is available to me, at any time, for my benefit. Although my doctors may not necessarily bring all their expertise or skill to bear on any one problem, they promise (by "hanging out a shingle") that if I fulfill certain conditions (detailed in the following chapters), they will do everything in their power to diagnose and treat whatever maladies I present. This promise includes a commitment to maintain our relationship until the treatment is completed. A good doctor will not quit in the middle of the healing agenda.

"Having" a doctor is not an exclusive arrangement for the doctor, since a doctor can have more than one patient. Nevertheless, our relationship still exists. There is no contradiction in saying that this person is my doctor and my wife's doctor as well. Neither is the "possession" restricted by time. My doctor is available to me twenty-four hours a day, to be used by me every day, several times a day if necessary. Although I may not consult my doctor for weeks or months or years, once I have established the relationship and have done what is necessary to maintain it, he or she is still "mine." My doctor's promises to treat me for my diseases are not negatively affected by other patients, the frequency of my need, or any other circumstances.

"Having" a doctor does not indicate servility, although my doctor promises to be my servant, in that all his or her skills will be put on the line for my benefit whenever I need them. I cannot order the doctor as I would a slave, nor can I think of myself as a superior being. Doctors who serve me do so because of their expertise and because of my inability to solve my problem on my own. In fact, because any doctor in this aspect of the relationship functions as a kind of lord, we must examine the concept of "lordship" if we are to more fully understand the essence of our connection with the Great Physician.

One kind of lordship could be labeled "employer lordship." This refers to the relationship that exists between an employer and an employee. The employer has a need that the employee fills. When the need is filled, the employer pays the employee a wage commensurate with the effort expended by the employee. The employer-lord instructs the employee about what needs to be done, and the employee usually lacks the freedom to disagree! An employee's responsibility is to do what the boss asks—or find another job. In this relationship the employer-lord maintains an image of superiority, so that the employee remains in a subordinate position in meeting the needs of the lord. A doctor does not exert *this* kind of lordship over a patient!

Another kind of lordship could be labeled "patron lordship" or "parental lordship." In such a relationship the patron/parent exercises authority over the client/child's behavior, even though the ultimate aim of the patron is the welfare of the client. The patron gives directions, which must be followed if the client wants to receive the benefits the patron promises, but the obedience the client renders brings rewards greater than the face value of the actions taken. When patrons exercise authority and commands, it is because they know what will bring about the best results for their clients. When a client obeys, he or she does so because of confidence that the patron will provide what has been promised. And when a client receives the benefit desired, the patron receives glory greater than the value of the "work" he has done. A good doctor exerts *this* kind of lordship over a patient!

A biblical comparison of these two kinds of lordship is found in the parable of the prodigal son and his gracious father, one of three parables in Luke 15 that center on the concept of repentance. The first two speak of God's joy over the repentance of sinners, and the third speaks of the kind of repentance God wants. In the prodigal's speech to himself he argues that he will go back and present himself to his father as one of the hired servants. He plans this approach because he no longer feels worthy to relate to his father as a son. But the father does not let him get very far into his speech of repentance. After running to embrace the prodigal, he cuts off his speech when he hears, "I am no longer worthy to be called your son," and goes out of his way to reward his repentance with much more than the sinner (or anyone else) might have reason to expect. (See Luke 15:11–32.)

In telling the last part of the parable, Jesus emphasizes the divine aversion to relating to his children on the tit-for-tat basis of employer-employee. The elder son is so angry at his father's graciousness that he refuses to imitate him, whining instead about the remuneration he has not received for all the work *he* has done for his father. Loving parents and patrons do reward the obedience of their children and clients, but not necessarily on a scale understandable to the recipient. This is true for two reasons. First, no advantage may accrue to the patron. When I obeyed my doctor's commands to exercise my back, he received no benefit for which I must be repaid in kind. Second, the benefit that the client receives does not correspond to the effort expended. My good health and overall well-being far outweigh the "value" of any amount of work I might expend toward that end.

In the doctor-patient analogy, God wants to be the patron and wants us to be the clients. In Jesus' father-child example, God wants to be the father and wants us to be his children. He does not regard the relationship as an employer-lordship. This conforms to what God told Adam and Eve in the Garden when he forbade them to partake of the tree of the knowledge of good and evil (possession of the ability to decide what is best for oneself, without reference to outside authority—see Deut. 1:39; 2 Sam. 14:17; 19:35; Isa. 7:15–16) and exhorted them to trust *him* for what they needed to know about what would be good for them. And it conforms to all the other parent-child images that God puts in Scripture alongside the King-subject images.

When we "have" a doctor, our relationship is with a patron-lord/parent-lord who employs wisdom and expertise for the benefit of all those who come with the intent of submitting themselves for his or her direction of their recovery process. So it is when we say that we "have" God as *our* god. When the Lord came to Abram and promised to be God to him, he offered to expend all his power and wisdom for Abram's benefit. Because of God's infinite and unique capabilities as a god, we designate him as GOD, to the exclusion of all other deities. The promise even implies the gift of eternal life, because God never placed limits on his willingness or ability to function as Abram's God. If Abram fulfilled the conditions set forth in the covenant, the Lord would be his God forever. So also will he be ours!

We are not surprised, when we come to the end of the Bible, to find the same language used as the Lord draws this age to a conclusion. As Paul reminds us, when we were "dead in our trespasses and sins," God, in his mercy, made us "alive together with Christ . . . in order that in the ages to come He might show the surpassing riches of His grace in kindness toward us in Christ Jesus" (Eph. 2:1–7).

When we "have" God as our doctor, we "have" the Creator-Ruler of the universe, graciously available to meet all our needs as he brings us along the road of recovery toward an eternity of joy in fellowship with the Father, Son, and Holy Spirit. Those who have the Son of God have the eternal life that he possesses. O that we might delight in having and holding the Great Physician, who loves us and saved us from the power and penalty of our previous refusals to let him care for us!

For *Reflection*

1. How have you been helped most by the concepts in this chapter?

2. How should knowing you are not working for God as an "employee" change the way you approach your day-to-day tasks?

3. What part of God's relating to you as "god" appeals to you most? Why?

5

For Goodness' Sake

If my people, concerning whom my reputation hangs in the balance, will humble themselves and pray and seek my face, then I will hear from heaven and will forgive their sin and will heal their land (2 Chron. 7:14 DWK).

Surely goodness and lovingkindness will pursue me all the days of my life, and I will dwell in the house of The Eternal God forever (Ps. 23:6 DWK).

If the Great Physician wants us to relate to him as a client relates to a patron or as a child relates to a parent, what does our life as a patient look like? Is there a term that will help us organize the many and varied attitudes and actions that compose our daily routines? What conditions must we fulfill that are necessary for maintaining the doctor-patient relationship between God and ourselves so we obtain the benefits he promises? What must we do so that we can say with accuracy, "The Lord is my God"?

Those who have a primary-care doctor have a better chance at staying healthy than those who don't. Expectant mothers who have regular prenatal care have smoother deliveries and healthier babies than those who don't. If you have a heart attack, you have a greater chance of survival and full recovery if you have a doctor than if you don't. Skiers who break their legs probably won't lose them (or their lives) to gangrene if they have a good orthopedist to supervise their treatment and recovery. In short, when injured or sick, having good doctors gives us hope for a good future, for they will do everything in their power to bring about our recovery, as long as we . . .

As long as we *what?* As patients we must have faith in our doctors. We must trust in the promises they make, based on their reputation. The same is true for our special relationship with the Great Physician. Faith is the hallmark of that relationship, too. It is the term that sums up the dynamics of our interaction. Faith on the part of the patient begins the relationship and keeps it going. If this condition is not filled, we patients can have no legitimate assurance that we will get well. We might talk about "our" doctor. We might go to the doctor's office and might even talk to the doctor. But until we actually form a working relationship with the doctor, he or she is not *our* doctor in the true sense of the word. Unless we have the *faith* that it is safe to put our very lives in this person's hands, we will not do what we must do to become healthy.

THE COMPLEXITY OF FAITH

We cannot talk about a "*simple* faith," because faith is complex. Faith is better compared to a chemical compound than to a single element. It is composed of a core element of confidence, to which are attached several other elemental affections. The faith that establishes a doctor-patient relationship is more than just acknowledging his or her ability. For us to be able to say with integrity that we "have" a certain doctor, we must enter a reciprocal relationship with this doctor that is characterized by a humble, loyal, enduring, joyful confidence on our part that the good he or she has promised will be accomplished.

Humility

The faith that retains a doctor is humble in that it looks away from what we can do for ourselves to what someone more capable can do for us. Putting our faith in the doctor is to recognize our own inability to diagnose or treat our problem, to admit that this person's knowledge and skills are superior to ours, and to apply for his or her direction and guidance. It means that we must accept someone else's definition of what is good for our lives, even if that seems to be radically different from our own assessment of the situation. Likewise, putting faith in the Great Physician entails a humble submission to his wisdom and will—doing the opposite of what Adam and Eve did when they first sinned!

In the Old Testament (2 Kings 5), we find the story of Naaman, the Aramean warrior who suffered from leprosy. His servant recommended that he consult Elisha, the man of God, so that he would be healed. After some delay, Naaman mounted his regiment, entered his chariot, and rode to find Elisha. When Naaman arrived at the prophet's door, Elisha sent a messenger with instructions for his cure. Naaman was furious that this great man of God did not come out to meet him personally. He was also furious with the manner of the cure: to dip himself seven times in the River Jordan! He expected that a man of his position deserved better treatment, so he decided that he would rather be sick than humble himself before the prophet and obey his instructions. But Naaman's servant argued with him about the foolishness of his response, saying, "If the prophet had told you to do some great thing [for which you could have been praised], would you not have done it? How much more then, when he says, 'Wash and be clean'" (2 Kings 5:13 DWK). Then Naaman humbled himself and followed the "doctor's" orders. After his healing he returned full of praise: "Now I know that there is no God in all the earth, but in Israel" (v. 15).

Loyalty

No doctor will continue to work wholeheartedly on our behalf if our faith does not also include the element of loyalty. Comparison shopping is reasonable while we are in the process of choosing a health-care provider. We want to be quite sure of the quality and reliability of our doctors before we commit ourselves to their care. However, once the choice is made, the doctor should be made to understand that we will be counting solely on him or her for the health benefits we desire. If we are not loyal, we imply that the doctor is not trustworthy, either morally or technically or both. If we are not loyal, we set ourselves up as equal to our doctor in medical knowledge, because we would have to know as much as any doctor in order to evaluate the differing opinions with which we might be presented. Disloyalty implies doubt on our part, and doctors cannot be totally committed to the care of patients who question their competence.

In view of the doctor-patient analogy we are applying to our relationship with God, it is appropriate to clarify some apparent differences between our loyalty to God and our loyalty to human doctors. First, none of them is infallible! Modern medicine is not yet a perfect art, so two equally competent physicians may hold differing opinions about either a diagnosis or a treatment plan. Even the doctor whom we trust wholeheartedly might suggest we seek a second opinion. Our insurance carrier might even require one, depending on the severity or complexity of our case. We are not being disloyal when we seek such knowledge. On the other hand, God has perfect knowledge and wisdom. Seeking an opinion from someone else would be disloyal to him.

Secondly, our human doctors also have a responsibility to inform us of all the options available to us. Asking them for all that information is not being disloyal. Because of the uncertainty inherent in all human medicine, there may seem to be more than one way to solve a problem. Our relationship with the Great Physician is similar in some ways. Even Jesus prayed three times in Gethsemane to see if there might be some other way to proceed. When he was certain of the best way, he recommitted himself completely into his Father's care. Once we are in the doctor-patient relationship concerning a certain disease and have chosen a treatment option, we must stop seeking other care-givers.

Thirdly, we may switch doctors depending on the disease we need treated. For appendicitis, we see a general surgeon. For skin cancer, a dermatologist. Doctors are limited in their expertise. So we are not disloyal if we seek an appropriate specialist for each individual problem. When we have a relationship with God, we do not need anyone else. He is truly omni-competent. So faith in God must be absolutely loyal, or it isn't faith. The conclusion of Naaman's story illustrates how important loyalty is.

After Naaman received his initial cure through Elisha, he ceased to trust the gods to whom he had previously been loyal and transferred his trust to the God of Israel. Because he knew that this transfer of faith included a promise on his part to be loyal to this one and only deity, at his conversion he talks through Elisha to God about what might seem to be an act of disloyalty: "When my master goes into the house of Rimmon to worship there, and he leans on my hand and I bow myself in the house of Rimmon" (2 Kings 5:18).

When he asks that "the LORD pardon your servant in this matter," Naaman begins to live according to the first of the Ten Commandments—"You shall have no other gods before Me" (Exod. 20:3)—and according to Jesus' teaching that we cannot expect to benefit from two masters (see Matt. 6:24). Only by placing our complete trust in the Great Physician can we achieve spiritual well-being.

Endurance

The story *King Rat,* by James Clavell, occurs in a prisoner-of-war camp in Southeast Asia during World War II. One of the friends of the story's hero becomes gravely ill. Medicines are surreptitiously obtained and treatment is begun, but with the doctor's warning that the treatment has to continue without interruption or the patient will die. Unfortunately, even today, doctors find that many people will not take a full course of antibiotics. As soon as they begin to feel better, they reason that they do not need the medicine any longer, in spite of what the doctor said. So they quit—and often suffer a relapse.

Notice what this says about the nature of faith. It must include the element of endurance. As soon as we stop following the doctor's instructions concerning our recovery plan, we have stopped trusting the doctor and begun thinking that we know what is best. If we do not endure in the treatment program, we show that we have more confidence in our own ability to prescribe our path to good health than in the doctor's.

In the realm of physical medicine, we might sometimes think we have a good reason for discontinuing a treatment—perhaps we have experienced unpleasant (and possibly dangerous) side effects that the doctor could not have anticipated. Even so, we must consult the doctor before giving up a medication or other regimen he or she had prescribed. To cease a treatment plan just because it causes us pain—physical, mental, or social—would be foolish. It would certainly manifest an unbelieving heart. Our faith lasts as long as we "endure" under the doctor's orders, once we learn that any discomfort is both temporary and unavoidable—as well it may be.

The Great Physician requires even greater endurance. Faith in God causes us to *continue* in his way unswervingly. The way is narrow and difficult. Along it we will experience pain, "But the one who endures to the end, he shall be saved" (Matt. 24:13; cf. Heb. 10:35–36). He calls us to a recovery program that presents great hardship but promises great benefits. The invitation to find rest for our souls assures that our labors will eventually cease and that we will have all burdens lifted from our hearts, but it does not promise that we will not have to exert effort or suffer pain in the process. We must take up our crosses daily and accompany Jesus wherever he leads. As we follow him we lay aside all claim to know the best way to proceed with our recovery from the disease of sin. We must endure to the end to receive the joy set before us: "Through many tribulations we must enter the kingdom of God" (Acts 14:22).

The Divine Doctor helps us attain the endurance he requires. Because he understands that our memory is short, he institutes means for helping us recall the goal of his treatment program. He also understands that we often get frustrated with the apparent slowness of our progress, so he provides awareness of the change that is taking place. When our emotional energy wanes, he presents us with pictures of the glorious state to which he will bring us in the end. He recognizes our fear of abandonment along the way and therefore makes clear to us that he is with us until the end of our struggle. When he promises to show us the pathway to eternity, where we will find fullness of joy and pleasures forever, we know that he cares for us very deeply. We endure because he soundly affirms that he will provide the continuity of care that we desperately crave.

The apostle Paul writes in his letter to the church at Philippi, "I thank my God in all my remembrance of you . . . in view of your participation in the gospel from the first day until now. For I am confident of this very thing, that He who began a good work in you will bring it to perfection at the day of Christ Jesus" (Phil. 1:3–6 DWK). God's purpose in reviving us from our spiritual death is that we might experience forever the outpouring of his glory and love in our lives. His purpose in making his plan so clear is that our hearts might be moved to continue in our allegiance to him, even when the treatment seems to be going nowhere.

Joy

Another element of faith that activates the doctor on behalf of the patient is a joyful confidence. The joy arises out of our anticipation of the goodness the doctor promises to help us attain. Many doctors who read this will think they know very few joyful patients. Their assessment is probably correct, as far as it goes, because the joy of faith does not occur as we deal with the circumstances of disease. Rather, that kind of joy occurs as we contemplate the promises the doctor makes and the likelihood of their fulfillment. Although this is true for spiritual as well as physical diseases, how much greater is our joyful confidence when the Great Physician is making those promises!

The joy of faith is both a joy of anticipation and a joy of celebration. The prospect of good health and resulting happiness held up to us by a trusted doctor makes us joyful. We can be glad that we now have hope, even though contemplation of our present situation may only bring sorrow and despair.

Furthermore, our joy nurtures the obedience our faith produces. As we look ahead to the good that our compliance with the doctor's orders will bring, we will be only too happy to do what we need to do, even if the obedience is painful. The joy is not in the pain, but in the promise. To David, God's commandments were a delight: "They are more desirable than gold, yes, than much fine gold. Sweeter also than honey and the drippings of the honeycomb" (Ps. 19:10) because they lead to a great reward (v. 11). When we joyfully obey, the Divine Doctor is pleased, because glad-hearted obedience honors him. Grudging, sour, angry, grit-your-teeth compliance is not part of honest faith, because it displays no real confidence in him.

Motivated Partnering

In the everyday world of health care, no medical or dental practitioner guarantees optimal results. Uncertainty is a reality of the profession. No one likes this, nor does anyone like to admit it, but uncertainty always exists for the clinician. It exists also in the mind of the patient in that none of us can ever be absolutely certain of the promised outcome. Nevertheless, we approach our doctors with at least a "mustard seed of faith." When we realize our need for a doctor, we look for someone who promises recovery and who looks capable of delivering on that promise. We go in faith to our doctors because we have reasonable assurance that they can guide us back to health. By virtue of retaining a particular doctor, we perceive that he or she is as motivated as we are in achieving that goal. In effect, we and our doctor are partners in seeking a better life—"goodness"—for us.

To help us be more certain, the Great Physician paints a clear picture of what will be true for us in the end. If we can imagine ourselves in that state, we will be more likely to continue on, no matter how difficult it becomes. In the Bible we find much that tells us how wonderful life will be when God removes all causes of disease and suffering. He shall "wipe away every tear" from our eyes, and there shall no longer be death. Mourning, crying, and pain will cease to exist, for "the first things have passed away" (Rev. 21:3–4). Indeed, we will be like the risen Christ, having "put on the incorruptible." We will have the same passionate love for the Father that he has for us. Because we will be totally free from the presence and power of sin in our lives, we will be able to love other people without shame and without reservation, and be able to receive the love of God unhindered. In our state of "goodness," we will enjoy the fellowship of the Father and the Son and the Holy Spirit, and do it in bodies that cannot be corrupted or destroyed.

The Great Physician also decreases our uncertainty by appealing to his past work on our behalf: "I am the LORD your God, who brought you out of the land of Egypt, out of the house of slavery. You shall have no other gods before Me" (Exod. 20:2–3). And Christ points to how he was sustained during his earthly ministry: "If you keep My commandments, you will abide in My love, just as I have kept My Father's commandments, and abide in His love" (John 15:10).

Human doctors routinely encourage us by showing progress reports in the form of X-ray pictures, test results, or microscopic evidence of change. If we are satisfied with what we are shown, we continue the treatment with renewed enthusiasm and hope. God also knows we must see change in our lives if we are to trust him to the end. So he tells us what changes should occur that will indicate genuine movement toward the wholeness and goodness he has promised. He also tells us about what does not necessarily indicate healing. For example, we know we are connected to Christ if we see answered prayer in our lives (see John 15:5–7). And we know we have "passed out of death into life," because we love other believers (1 John 3:14). When we see such fruit, our uncertainty decreases.

Obviously, we are strongly motivated to maintain the partnership or working relationship with our doctors and to do what they say. We go to a doctor because we see him or her as a somewhat secure and stable source of joy regarding our physical well-being. Since security and stability are necessary to our happiness, they are strong motivators. Otherwise, we would worry that somehow what works for our "good" could be taken away from us capriciously or that our potential source of joy might fall apart on us. A secure and stable dispenser of promised joy will leave us no anxiety. When we talk about doctors being "sources of joy," we mean they are people who can work for the happiness we obtain when we have good health, even though their abilities do not extend to other areas in our lives.

On the other hand, the Great Physician is the absolutely secure and stable source of joy for *every* facet of our being. In him we live and move and have our identity forever. Besides him there is no other. He always uses his perfect power to act according to what his infinite wisdom shows him is best. The righteous God created us and knows us intimately. When we recognize our need for him and see him for who he is and what he can do, we are then absolutely sure that the eternal goodness he promises will bring us all the joy we could ever hope to obtain. By grace he promises to deliver us from the penalty and power of sin in our lives, making us people who are incorruptibly dedicated to experiencing fullness of joy in his presence, where pleasures are forever available from his generous hand.

For goodness' sake we ought to make sure we have the Triune God of the Bible as our god. No other god will work for our good nor be a secure and stable source of joy. Money, sex, power, prestige, fast cars, strong bodies, fine families—or anything else we crave—fail to provide peace and happiness. For none of these things is permanent enough to free us from anxiety about our future.

For goodness' sake we must joyfully seek the Father—the only one who can release us from the wrath we deserve for trying to substitute other objects of worship. *For goodness' sake* we ought to seek our satisfaction in Christ Jesus, the Savior who works as a patron-lord on our behalf. *For goodness' sake* we ought to gladly seek the presence of the Holy Spirit, who can fill our hearts with the love for the Father and the Son that is experienced in the Trinity. *For goodness' sake* call on the Great Physician. He is always available, eager, and willing to answer all our questions and to sustain us on our pilgrimage to eternal joy.

For *Reflection*

1. How would you respond to someone who says, "We must not ask God to do too much for us"?

2. Based on what you have read here, how would you explain to a friend the relationship between what Jesus did while he was on earth and what he does for us now from heaven?

3. Describe situations in which one element of faith (as described in this chapter) was more prominent than the others.

6

A.P.T.A.T.—
Stat!

"... Christ lives in me; and the life which I now live in the flesh I live by faith in the Son of God, who loved me, and delivered Himself up for me" (Gal. 2:20).

Without becoming weak in faith he [Abraham] contemplated his own body, now as good as dead ... yet, with respect to the promise of God, he did not waver in unbelief but grew strong in faith, giving glory to God (Rom. 4:19–20).

I n the previous chapter we looked at the nature of the faith we must have if we want to say with heartfelt assurance that God is *our* "doctor." We saw that faith always exists in a relationship of promises. When we have faith we promise to entrust our future to the person who makes certain promises to us. When doctors establish a practice, they promise the public that whoever calls on them for medical care will receive the doctors' best efforts on his or her behalf *if* the patient will promise to obey the doctors' directives. The person of faith answers a promise of help with a promise of obedience. This "obedience of faith" (see Rom. 1:5; 16:26) allows a patient of the Great Physician to participate in all the goodness the divine healer has to offer.

What does this look like as we encounter life's wide variety of circumstances? How do we battle against the alternatives we confront each day that seem more attractive than God's prescription for us? What can we do to make it easier to act in a way that springs from faith in his promises? Many situations are especially challenging or threatening, so that acts of obedience and service could be dangerous or embarrassing. Or there may be times when we must withstand great temptation if potential good is to be the outcome. In other words, how do we approach and enter the stressful or exciting arenas of life so that we ourselves are helped, other people are served, and the Great Physician gets the glory?

The Bible approaches the answer to this question from several different angles, but they all point to a workable solution that keeps us focused on the promises God secured for us through Jesus' work on our behalf. For example, Paul tells us he lives "by faith in the Son of God, who loved me and delivered Himself up for me" (Gal. 2:20). This means we are to rest in what Jesus accomplished through his incarnation and crucifixion and look forward to the grace he has ready for us when we need it. Through him we have access to the Father, both for forgiveness and for mercy and grace in our time of need.

Another slant on how to confront the issues of life is found in the command to "walk by the Spirit" (see Gal. 5:16). When we live this way, we will not gratify the appetites of the flesh—those self-centered, self-exalting cravings for personal autonomy. The promises of Scripture come by inspiration of the Holy Spirit and paint a

picture of how life on his holy path is much more delightful than what anything or anybody else can offer. So
"walking by the Spirit" must involve our interaction with
the commands and promises of Scripture.

Living the Christian life means extending the grace we
receive through Jesus to others "by the strength which
God supplies; so that in all things God may be glorified
through Jesus Christ . . ." (1 Peter 4:11). Peter doesn't
mean physical strength in this case, although God supplies that also. He means the strength of will that occurs
when our hearts are overcome by the beauty and joy of
God's goodness to us, especially as we see it in his Word.
"The joy of the LORD is your strength" (Neh. 8:10) means
that God has promised us the good we need so we will
have enough to be as joyfully generous as he is.

The promises of God are the common thread in all
three of these examples. It follows that there is a simple way of approaching the contingencies of life to demonstrate and validate our relationship with the Divine
Doctor. Each step of this way fulfills his conditions and
keeps us in a position to benefit from his work for us.
Whether we are confronting an antagonist, consulting
with a difficult client, considering how to tell someone
about Christ, evaluating a contract, disciplining a child,
choosing a new car, or loving an enemy, we have an
effective way to live. When the day is done, we will be
able to say with integrity, "I lived by faith, walked by the
Spirit, and served in God's strength. To him be the
glory."

One way to outline this lifestyle is called A.P.T.A.T. The
acronym was developed by the pastoral staff at Bethle-
hem Baptist Church in Minneapolis, Minnesota. It con-
sists of five steps, each of which keeps us looking to the
wisdom and power of the Divine Doctor for success in
overpowering the pockets of sin-infection that still trouble us.

THE A.P.T.A.T. PROGRAM

Step One: ADMIT that without Christ we are helpless and at risk

None of us can please God, live by faith, walk by the Spirit, or serve in God's strength until we admit our utter helplessness without Christ our Lord—physically, morally and spiritually. Our vulnerability occurs on at least five levels that we need to recognize and admit from our hearts.

1. *We owe our beginning to the work of Christ.* "He was in the beginning with God; all things were made through him, and without him was not anything made that was made" (John 1:2–3 DWK). The inception of a human being involves more than just the joining of strands of DNA. It involves the intimate, imaginative, sovereign act of the Creator.

2. *Our continued existence is dependent entirely upon the grace of God.* We would vanish out of existence without the moment-by-moment sustaining work of Christ. "He is before all things, and in Him all things hold together" (Col. 1:17). God gives to all men life and breath and everything else (see Acts 17:25). Every breath we take we owe to Christ. We are utterly helpless without his sustenance and support.

3. *We would have no true virtue without Christ's work in our souls.* "The natural man [i.e., the man without the Spirit of Christ] does not welcome the things of the Spirit of God, for they are folly to him. Indeed, he is not able to see their significance because they are spiritually evaluated" (1 Cor. 2:14 DWK). "I will give you a new heart and put a new spirit within you. . . . And I will put My Spirit within you and cause you to walk in My statues, and you will be careful to observe My ordinances" (Ezek. 36:26–27). Until the Spirit of God invades our soul and gives us a spiritual

thirst, we recoil at spiritual things and reject what the Divine Doctor is telling us to do. It follows that we are utterly helpless to love God and live for his sake without the renovating power of Christ.

4. *Without the biblical word of God, we would not know what constitutes a righteous, healthy lifestyle.* The Lord has told us what to do. There are hundreds of specific commands in Scripture and many more implied imperatives. When we hear the laws of God taught in the "clinics" we call church, or when we read them in the Bible, we do not see impossibilities set before us. Rather, these are his loving instructions, the guidelines by which our confidence in him is to be demonstrated. Without his direction we would lose our way.

5. *Without Christ's enablement, we are helpless to bring forth any results from our lives that are significant in the sense that God is glorified.* By the world's standards, we might accomplish many noteworthy things *without* Christ. We might make a large charitable contribution to a good cause, discover a much-needed vaccine, or design a cheap, pollution-free transportation device. But, from God's perspective, without Christ we are like shriveled barren twigs: "I am the vine, you are the branches; he who abides in Me, and I in him, he bears much fruit; *for apart from Me you can do nothing*" (John 15:5, emphasis added).

So, Step One as we face the tasks of our lives is to admit our helplessness by praying: "O Lord, I can't do anything without you. Without Christ, I wouldn't exist; I couldn't take another breath. If I weren't known and loved by you, I could bear no fruit for your glory." This act of great humility is where living by faith begins. King Solomon began following the Divine Doctor's prescription for him to govern a great nation by praying for help. He admitted his helplessness without the empowerment of God and received exactly the strength and wisdom he needed. The apostle Paul had the same sense of inadequacy:

"Such confidence we have through Christ toward God. Not that we are adequate in ourselves to consider anything as coming from ourselves, but our adequacy is from God" (2 Cor. 3:4–5). With faith in the grace of God, walking by the Spirit begins with the conscious admission of our inability to do what the Lord has prescribed unless he empowers us.

Step Two: PRAY for God's help

A "day of trouble" (Ps. 77:2) has many faces. It is the time when we realize that we are involved in a difficult situation that will require something extra if we are to succeed. We might be facing a new job or a difficult business negotiation. Perhaps we are about to talk to a friend about Christ. It could be when we need to reprimand an employee wisely or respond lovingly to an angry child. Whether it happens in the car, in the office, at school, or at home, when a challenge seems too tough, our first thought should be to admit that without Christ nothing good will come of any of our efforts. Then we should pray very simply and very humbly: "Help me, O God! Please help me!" Our requests might be more specific:

"Help me not to forget anything important."
"Help me to be wise in my response."
"Help me to be gracious enough to accept the bad news without grumbling."
"Help me to love this person and not be bitter."
"Help me not to forget whose I am."

These prayers are all calls to the Great Physician for assistance.

King Jehosaphat modeled this idea when he led the people of Judah in a prayer of desperation: "We are powerless before this great multitude who are coming against us; nor do we know what to do, but our eyes are on you" (2 Chron. 20:12). And David let the Lord know his need in a most difficult, yet ordinary, circumstance when he asked for help in setting a guard over his mouth so he wouldn't say anything foolish.

Even when God gives us a new heart that is able to comprehend the nature of the reality of sin in our lives, we do not become instantly strong. That takes practice in discerning good and evil (see Heb. 5:14). But we are at least able to recognize our weaknesses and therefore our need for the aid of a spiritual doctor. In fact, God *commands* us to seek his strong help in time of need: "Call upon Me in the day of trouble; I shall rescue you, and you will honor Me" (Ps. 50:15). It is essential for Christian living that we admit our need and seek strength and help from God through Jesus Christ.

When you ask, "How shall I live so that I get help and God gets the glory?" the answer starts in these first two steps: *Admit* your need and *Pray* for help. This doesn't mean that the Lord will always help in the way that we demand or expect, but that in our weakness he will do what is necessary for us to accomplish the purpose to which he has called us. "My grace is sufficient for you, for power is perfected in weakness" (2 Cor. 12:9) is God's answer to Paul's prayer for help—so that Paul could say with conviction, "When I am weak, then I am strong" (v. 10).

Step Three: TRUST in an appropriate promise of God

All the issues of life are issues of faith, in that every choice we make demonstrates whether or not we have confidence in the living God. This is what Paul meant when he said, ". . . Christ lives in me; and the life which I now live . . . I live by faith in the Son of God" (Gal. 2:20). Living by faith means overcoming any obstacles to obedience by *trusting* God's promises for help and future happiness.

When human physicians prescribe a regimen of chemotherapy to stop the growth of a cancerous tumor, there is an implied promise that if the patient will persevere in the treatment, the tumor will disappear and his or her life will be spared. It is the hope engendered by this promise that keeps the patient going for treatments, in spite of loss of hair and general malaise due to the process. This is "living by faith." Moses lived this way when he chose "to endure ill-treatment with the people of God, [rather] than to enjoy the passing pleasures of sin," because "he was looking to the reward" (Heb. 11:26–27). Of course, even the most qualified human doctor cannot always guarantee success of a treatment plan. But the Great Physician—he whose promises can be totally relied upon—will not disappoint us.

An act is an act of faith in God when the strength to do it comes through trusting in one of his promises. When we bank our hope on God's help and the happiness he promises, we gain the strength we need to get us through any task he assigns us. We are living by faith and walking by the Spirit.

Every day we are confronted with choices—to do right or wrong, to be honest or dishonest, to be loving or indifferent, to forgive or go on holding a grudge, to speak of Christ or be silent, to do an assignment or put it off, to follow God's leading to the mission field or stay home. And there are always obstacles to making the right choice: fear, pride, discouragement, addiction to comfort. Because all these come in many forms and intensities, we must be alert to what God has told us.

Living by faith is not passive. It involves energetic, disciplined tactical maneuvers on the spiritual battleground. If time and circumstances permit, we can go to our Bibles and look for some promise suited to our specific challenge. For example, if we are struggling to let go of a grudge and forgive our enemy, we can refer to Romans 12:17–19: "Never pay back evil for evil. . . . be at peace with all men. . . . leave room for the wrath of God, for it is written, 'Vengeance is Mine, I will repay,' says the Lord." Or consider Jesus' words in Matthew 6:14–15: "If you forgive men for their transgressions, your heavenly Father will also forgive you. But if you do not forgive men, then your Father will not forgive your transgressions." Such passages will help us see the benefit of forgiveness and that God will settle accounts far more justly and fairly than we ever could.

Or, if we are struggling with covetousness, we can go to James 4:1–6, which ends with the Old Testament promise that "God is opposed to the proud, but gives grace to the humble." Hebrews 13:5–6 is also helpful in this regard:

> Let your character be free from the love of money, being content with what you have. For He Himself has said, "I will never desert you, nor will I ever forsake you." So that we confidently say, "The Lord is my helper, I will not fear. What shall man do to me?"

Of course there are occasions when we do not have time to look through the Bible for a tailor-made guarantee. So, to bolster our trust, we all need to have an arsenal of general promises ready to use whenever an attitude of unbelief threatens to lead us astray from God's commands. Here are a few proven weapons:

> "Fear not, for I am with you. Be not dismayed, for I am your God. I will help you. I will strengthen and help you. I will uphold you by My righteous right hand" (Isa. 41:10 DWK).

> He who did not spare His own Son, but delivered Him up for us all, how will He not also with Him freely give us all things? (Rom. 8:32).

[Jesus said:] "All authority has been given to Me in heaven and on earth. . . . and, lo, I am with you always, even to the end of the age" (Matt. 28:18, 20).

How encouraging it is to our sagging spirits to know that the Lord of the universe is just as much with us today as he was with his disciples during his earthly ministry:

[God has said:] "Call upon Me in the day of trouble; I shall rescue you, and you will honor Me" (Ps. 50:15).

And my God shall supply all your needs according to His riches in glory in Christ Jesus (Phil. 4:19).

Constantly adding to our arsenal of promises is mandatory. We should repeatedly look for a new one to take with us through each day. Then, if an hour of challenge and trial comes, we will have the spiritual nitroglycerin that will protect our hearts from self-destruction. We will receive the strength to do right if we *Trust* a promise from the Word of God that suits our situation.

Step Four: ACT with humble confidence in God's help

This step may seem obvious, but we need to mention it as necessary in the process. There are some who say that since Christ lives through us, *we* should not have to do anything. That is, we simply wait passively until we are carried along by his will. But this is not at all what Scripture teaches. The Spirit of God does not cancel our will nor remove the need for us to act. Rather, the Spirit transforms our will, and God works in us, *so that* we can work. Paul argues, ". . . work out your salvation with fear and trembling, for it is God who is at work in you, both to will and to work for His good pleasure" (Phil. 2:12–13).

When we have *Admitted* to God that we can do nothing without him, *Prayed* for his help, and *Trusted* his promises, then we must move ahead. We must *Act!* And in so doing, we will be helped, others will be served, and God will get the glory.

Step Five: THANK *God for the good that comes*

We began with prayer in our admission of need and followed this with a cry for help. We end with prayer, too. This is what will come if serving "by the strength which God supplies" (1 Peter 4:11) has really happened in our lives. Since God gives the help, God should get the glory, which begins with our thanksgiving. This is why Paul's command in Colossians 3:17 makes sense: "And whatever you do in word or deed, do all in the name of the Lord Jesus, giving thanks through Him to God the Father." When we receive the grace to pursue a course of action in the name of the Lord—that is, for *his* glory and by faith in *his* promises—we should give thanks to God. If the person to whom we are witnessing experiences a change of heart, we should also thank God. It is the Great Physician who changes hearts and injects us with good intentions. An abundance of thanks gives glory to God.

STAT!

Although patients of the Great Physician are in the best of health-care programs, we should never presume on his good graces by living as though we had been completely healed from our disease of sinfulness. Full recovery will not be ours until we receive resurrection bodies and all the agents of spiritual illness are eradicated. Until then, we must learn to live a moment at a time, remembering that "The only easy day was yesterday!"

Emergency teams responding to critical medical situations have a code word for "Carry out the instructions I gave you—immediately and with all due speed." That word is *stat.* It comes from the Latin *statim* which means "at once" or "immediately." When we face a challenge or a temptation we must operate with the same urgency. We must:

A: ADMIT that without Christ we are helpless and at risk.
P: PRAY for God's help.
T: TRUST in an appropriate promise of God.
A: ACT with humble confidence in God's help.
T: THANK God for the good that comes.

   Stat!

For *Reflection*

1. Find some promises in Scripture that will help you obey the Lord's commands regarding:

   Cynicism

   Anxiety

   Purity

   Patience

2. What steps must you take to make these patterns of behavior your regular way of living?

7

Let Me Tell You...

For who is our hope or joy or crown of exultation? Is it not even you, in the presence of our Lord Jesus at His coming? For you are our glory and joy (1 Thess. 2:19–20).

[Jesus said to the man healed of demon-possession:] "Return to your house and describe what great things God has done for you." And he went away, proclaiming throughout the whole city what great things Jesus had done for him (Luke 8:39).

One of the natural results of a successful relationship between patient and doctor is the patient's motivation to refer others to the doctor. Physicians don't require it of us as a condition for treatment, though they probably expect it. The need to spread the news of our improved health arises partly from our sense of satisfaction with all the doctor has done. It increases our joy when we share that joy with someone else. Such a celebration allows us to re-experience the original joy and contrast it with our previous discomfort. When we bring someone else into this circle of joy, we are commending the doctor's success and hoping that others will retain his or her services when the need arises.

This "need" to communicate our good fortune does not arise out of emptiness, as some needs often do. It is more like the energy that impels a fountain to overflow. Similarly, a river's urge to flow onward is an indicator of its continuing fullness. But this analogy may be too impersonal. The impulse to bring someone else into the fellowship of our joy in our physician is something like how I feel when I've seen a beautiful sunset all by myself. I can hardly wait to tell my wife! The more beautiful the sunset, the greater the sense of urgency. The general principle is that if we prize some person or experience or object highly, we feel strongly compelled to express our praise to someone else. Our delight with our human doctors and what they have helped to accomplish in our lives frees us to talk enthusiastically about them.

David epitomizes this kind of urgent praise when he writes: "People shall speak of the power of your awesome acts, and I will tell of your greatness. They shall bubble over with the memory of your abundant goodness and will sing joyfully of your righteousness" (Ps. 145:6–7 DWK).

Besides the compulsion to express our joy, there is a certain implied obligation to our neighbors that causes us to make a medical "referral." Some of our obligations come from the promises to return resources to those who have loaned them to us. Other debts occur when we discover resources so vast that we would be vilified if we kept them to ourselves. When we tell a friend about our doctor because we've heard our friend has contracted the same set of symptoms our doctor helped us overcome, we are operating out of this kind of responsibility.

We find the clearest biblical example of this in 2 Kings. The army of the king of Aram had besieged the city of Samaria for so long that the people were beginning to resort to cannibalism (see 6:26–29). Four lepers debated whether to enter the city and die there from hunger or defect to the Arameans and take their chances. They decided to seek the mercy of the enemy, but when they reached the camp, it was deserted. The Arameans had fled when the Lord caused them to hear "the sound of a great army" (2 Kings 7:6). The lepers found food, weapons, clothes, and money—tent after tent of it—so they helped themselves. Soon, however, they realized that something was wrong: "Then they said to one another, 'We are not doing right. This day is a day of good news, but we are keeping silent; if we wait until morning light, punishment will overtake us. Now therefore come, let us go and tell the king's household'" (7:9).

We have the same kind of indebtedness concerning our relationship with the Great Physician. Paul voiced this when he argued, "I am under obligation both to Greeks and to barbarians, both to the wise and to the foolish. Thus, for my part, I am eager to preach the gospel to you also who are in Rome" (Rom. 1:14–15). He felt two kinds of pressure. He was eager to spread the good news because of his joy, and he was compelled because of the Romans' need for what God could do for them. It was only reasonable for him to feel this way, for God had displayed his power in Paul's life so clearly that he was absolutely unashamed to proclaim the message that God is able to deliver *anyone* from the grip of sin.

Since what the Great Physician can do for us is so far beyond what any human doctor can do, our enthusiastic recommendation of him to others becomes absolutely imperative. When Paul says, ". . . I am under compulsion; for woe is me if I do not preach the gospel" (1 Cor. 9:16), he is talking about more than his special calling as an apostle. Neglecting to recommend the Divine Doctor to others is to indicate we are not really very happy with what he has done for us, or are unappreciative of what he promises us in the future. It implies that we do not approve of his purpose in healing us.

Unlike most human physicians, who make us well so we can return to whatever lives we were leading prior to our illnesses, God heals us so we will move on to something better. His purpose for our physical and spiritual healing is to bless us so we can extend his goodness to others. The task of human doctors is ultimately futile, since every patient they treat will eventually succumb to physical death. In a sense, they are wasting their time and only putting off the inevitable. If they practice medicine only to return their patients to a self-destructive, god-debasing life, they are to be pitied more than praised. God is not so foolish. He heals us so we can experience the joy of being free from the penalty of sin now and eventually live as he intended all people to live when he created us, fully enjoying the glory of his goodness.

It follows that our relationship with the Great Physician creates a need to tell others about how wonderful he is and how much they will enjoy having him as their healer, too. It may be helpful to talk to them in terms of this very analogy. How you begin depends on the situation, and the analogy can be brought into the conversation at several different points. However you introduce the subject, everyone will feel most comfortable if you remember to describe the discussion as a "referral" to someone whom you have found to be very helpful in your life.

One way to pique a person's interest is to say something like, "Lately I've been thinking how much my relationship with Christ is like my relationship with my doctor. Has it ever occurred to you how God works for us in a way similar to our doctors?" Your friend will probably respond in the negative and may even ask what you mean. So you could reply, "First, what would you say are the characteristics of a good doctor?" Asking this question helps in several ways: It leads into a discussion rather than a one-sided lecture. Your friend's answer gives you tacit approval to continue along this line of thought. As you receive clues about the way someone thinks of doctors, you will be able to argue more persuasively. Adapting your understanding of God as the Great Physician to the peculiar emphases of other people does not weaken your position. Instead, it makes it easier for them to wrap their minds around what you say. If you then share from your experience and from Scripture how the Lord has made a difference in your life—highlighting the way each of his characteristics was used to bring about change—you can close the discussion by asking your audience if they, too, would like that transforming experience.

Another way to get listeners interested in the Great Physician is to speak of the connection between the human heart and disease. In spiritual terms, we defined the human "heart" earlier as "the faculty of the soul where our affections dwell, our plans are evaluated, and our commitments are made." Since the unchanged heart is proud, stubborn, and resistant to God's ways, it loves what is harmful, pursues what is worthless, and either hangs onto what is hopeless or easily runs from what is helpful. In the process, medical science confirms, we put ourselves in harm's way. Human choices that flow from a self-centered approach to life often cause us to become physically diseased. For example, sexually transmitted diseases affect millions worldwide. Studies show that divorce puts both men and women at greater risk of suffering circulatory problems—high blood pressure, heart attack, and stroke—and of contracting infections of many kinds. Even such injuries as broken bones often occur after our pride induces us to take dangerous risks.

It's not easy trying to make the jump from treating physical ailments to dealing with spiritual disease. The following is a true account of a conversation between a senior resident and his professor that occurred while doing rounds in the wards of a West London hospital, near a red-light district.

> The resident wrote in a letter that four female patients—apparently prostitutes—were seen in various stages of chronic pelvic inflammatory disease. Each of the women gave their medical history, using words like, "Life has been hell," "I have pain," "I have had terrible periods," or "I am sterile." Once the histories were presented, the professor remarked, "My job is to get these girls physically well so that they can go back to having a good time."
>
> The senior resident replied, "Excuse me, sir, but what do you mean by 'having a good time'?"
>
> "Well, you know."
>
> "I am sorry, I do not know."
>
> "Well, oh, come on, come on."
>
> "Well, I don't know, sir! We've just heard their stories. One said that life was 'hell' so I don't see how going back to it can possibly be fun. They have gotten this disease from having casual sexual relations, and if they return to that lifestyle, things are certainly not going to get better. So what they need to be told is 'Stop it! You need to change your behavior'"
>
> "Come on," the professor replied, "you are being judgmental; you are moralizing. It is not part of a doctor's role to do that."
>
> *What a shame,* thought the resident.

The strategy this resident advocates is a variation of the one Jesus used throughout much of his ministry. The Bible is full of incidents in which he demonstrated the power of the kingdom of God by healing people of their physical diseases, but he made it clear that his primary mission was to deliver people from their sin. For example, when a paralytic's friends brought him to Jesus, all Jesus did at first was declare the man's sins forgiven. After the religious leaders accused him of blasphemy, Jesus asked them a question, "Which is easier, to say to the paralytic, 'Your sins are forgiven'; or to say, 'Arise, and take up your pallet and walk'?" Jesus had done the difficult task, the task only God could do. To show that he had the authority to do what he did, he also healed the paralytic (see Mark 2:1–12). Healing of physical disease symptoms is a parable that illustrates the broader concept of spiritual healing of the effects of sin in our lives.

We can direct our conversation in ways similar to Jesus. Whether or not people in our audience are actually ill, we can ask them questions that will help them see their need of someone to care for their "heart." For instance, after talking for a few minutes about stories in the media linking disease to lifestyle, say, "I can't help thinking as we speak that what many of us really need is a doctor for our hearts. Don't you think we would see a lot less disease if our hearts were truly healthy? What I mean is, wouldn't we be better off if our thoughts and motivations were more wholesome and less self-centered?" By phrasing it this way, it doesn't sound like an attack, because it includes *yourself* in the block of humanity being considered. If another person seems receptive, the next part of this interchange gets personal: Mention a time when your own sinful attitude got you into a situation that resulted in an illness. Then ask if your friend has ever experienced anything similar. After you hear the other's story ask, "What did you do to change the way you were living?"

Depending on how things go at this point, you want to watch for an opportunity to ask, "I'd like to tell you how

I was able to change my heart. Would you be willing to hear my story?" Then you can talk about how forgiveness is available in a relationship with the Great Physician, and how trusting his prescriptions for your life made all the difference. Emphasize the truth of John 12:25: If you hang on to the life you've made apart from God, you'll lose it; but if you put all that behind you and exchange it for what God holds out to you, you'll really have something to hold on to, *forever.* End by recommending Jesus to your friend. Be ready, too, to extend your outreach further. Offer to help this person learn more about the Lord—perhaps by setting up future discussion times or extending an invitation to attend church or a Bible study with you.

You will succeed in this effort to the extent that you can offer good evidence of the Divine Doctor's work in your own life. If your recommendations are merely academic exercises, their inauthenticity will be evident. If your enthusiasm is not genuine, who will believe you are truly happy with the Lord? If you are so strongly convinced that his prescription for living is the only one that makes sense, that it offers everyone the absolutely best possible future, and that we should forsake all the spiritual quacks and charlatans we encounter, you will have no trouble "doing right by" the Great Physician and recommending him to the world around you.

For *Reflection*

1. How does this concept of evangelism change the way you feel when you think of telling someone else about Jesus?

2. Explain to someone else the different kinds of "need" discussed in this chapter.

3. What great things has the Lord done for you that will motivate you to refer him to others who need his help?

Epilogue

[Jesus said:] "Go and report to John what you have seen and heard: the blind receive sight, the lame walk, the lepers are cleansed, and the deaf hear, the dead are raised up, the poor have the gospel preached to them. And blessed is he who keeps from stumbling over Me" (Luke 7:22–23).

Misperceptions of Christ abound. Even John the Baptist was not certain at first if Jesus was the one whose coming he was appointed to announce.

We've all heard about or talked to someone who says, "I admire Jesus. He was a good teacher."

We reply, "Oh? What did he teach that made him seem so good to you?"

"Love."

"Really? Tell you what, think of the person who you believe dislikes you the most, someone who thinks of you as the lowest of the low, the scum of the earth, and has treated you badly. Now imagine seeing him walk down the street. Watch in your mind as three hoodlums grab him, pull him into an alley, rob him, beat him, and leave him for dead. How do you feel? Got what's coming to him, right? Not according to Jesus. Jesus would have you step into the picture, find the man, get him to a hospital, arrange for his care, pay his medical bills, and come back later to check up on him. That's the 'love' Jesus taught. Is that why you think Jesus is a good teacher?"

Another misperception about Christ and our relationship with him is that obedience is an optional addition to our faith. "It's good but not necessary for salvation" is one way we encounter this. Or we might hear, "To be a Christian all you have to do is believe that Jesus died for our sins." This mistaken idea causes problems by forcing people to split their thinking and talking into two categories: faith and obedience. We hear about both qualities, but seldom does anyone connect them accurately.

That kind of erroneous thinking is why this book had to be written. The doctor-patient analogy shows us how faith and obedience are inextricably linked. Talking about one without tying it to the other rends the fabric of Scripture and causes Christians to become spiritual schizophrenics. On the other hand, knowing how and why faith and obedience fit together allows us to pursue the fellowship of heaven as whole people. We can avoid the perils of legalism on one side and lawlessness on the other when we are able to talk and think as Jesus did. He told us that the one who *believes* in him has eternal life, but also that the one who does not *obey* him will experience the wrath of God. With that in mind, we are able to engage in evangelism and missions with a single goal: to bring about the obedience of faith. That is the only goal consistent with Jesus' command to make disciples—as opposed to the too-frequent modern practice of getting people to make "decisions" to receive Jesus as Savior and then *hoping* they will also make him Lord. Accepting Jesus as our personal Divine Doctor means submitting to him as the patron-lord who will save us as we follow him in the obedience of faith.

I pray, now that you have finished reading, that this concept has so commended itself to your heart and mind that you will think more deeply and search more diligently into its truth. I hope that, like your experience with a new car, you suddenly see the details of this model on every page of Scripture. I trust that as you work out the implications of this paradigm in your day-to-day experience, the Great Physician will enable you to sense and experience in full measure the wonderful healing that comes in his care.